The Indigo Psalms

Vol I

I.A. Rogers

Word of Life

You, my Lord,
Are my energy & my life,
Your word is my light & sustains me in every way,
You fill every breath I breathe,
Joy swells in my heart.
Your word is my treasure,
Your thoughts I meditate on.
I praise you all day long,
I talk to you & listen.
You are my rock & my shield,
My fortress to where I run,
I am safe because I am in the presence of the almighty,
I rest because I am under the shadow of his wings.
You calm my troubled heart,
& still my reeling thoughts,
To you alone I yield.
I do not fear for I am yours,
You have chosen me.
You do not fail.
Your faithfulness & justice never end,
Your glory shines throughout all generations.
Each day you make me anew,
Each day you restore my soul,
You alone can fill me.
Lord, your word is my weapon,
Destroyer of the enemy,
Sharper than any two-edged sword.
You, oh Lord, are my life & my energy,
& no one can extinguish this fire.

First

Though my body is broken,
I rejoice,
Though my flesh fades,
I sing your praises.
For though I am cast out,
I am welcomed,
Though I am abandoned,
I am not alone.
For although people exclude me,
& war against me,
I am found in the highest dwelling place.
If they hate me for his name's sake,
I can be glad of it,
For he was first hated for me.

How Long?

How long, oh Lord, how long?
How long must I wait?
I eagerly anticipate your promises,
The good things you've destined for me.
I long for this dream you've given me to come to pass.
I fervently await its arrival.
Lord, I trust your timing.
I will trust you in the waiting.
May I not get impatient,
May I not fall away.

Peace

Lord, your mercy & grace never cease.
Your love, so high I cannot attain it.
You speak just a single word, & my soul is filled,
My heart swells to overflow.
Such love, so deep & wide,
So undeserved yet freely given.
Just a slight breath & your peace flows through me like a river,
So cool, refreshing, & soothing.
I rest in your forever strong yet gentle arms,
I know I am safe.
You are with me,
There is nothing I will fear.
You are near me,
There is nothing of which I will be afraid.

Untainted Love

Lord, my voice cracks & I break,
But every time I fall, you lift me up.
You hold me close & whisper, 'You are mine.'
My soul melts at your tenderness,
Your love, so pure, perfect, & full,
Yet so undeserved.
What more could I want for,
Than this love, so deep & constant?
What else could I long for,
More than this sure, untainted love?

Help Me See

Right now, I don't feel like praising you,
I don't want to shout for joy.
Anger eats me up,
Hopelessness & despair cloud my mind.
I don't want to be in this world,
Nor do I want to be of it!
I just want to be with you,
But right now, I can't see.
Where is the 'good' in your 'good world'?
I look around & cannot find it.
It looks like once again,
Hopelessness & despair blind me.
Lord, help me look to you,
Let the scales drop from my eyes.
Remove this blinding smoke,
& help me see your goodness.

Heavenward

Upward I gaze at the night sky,
The vastness & beauty of your creation overwhelms me.
How stars; raging balls of lava & gas,
Are likened to glitter on a dark velvet robe.
Such beauty & soothing calm,
Yet such power, fury & chaos.
I look back to earth with a sinking heart,
So much pain is inflicted here.
True, much joy is wrought as well,
But the pain often feels impossible to bear.
Lord, help me keep my eyes heavenward,
For when I look down, sadness & anger threaten to drown me.
You alone are peace in this chaos.
You alone are our hope.
Without you there is no good.

Way, Truth, Life

You are the way.
Although the path seems lonely & narrow,
You guide my every step; you are with me.

You are the truth.
You cannot lie,
That means that when you say you love me,
It is full, complete, unconditional love.
When you make a promise,
You keep it.
You are the complete fullness of truth.

You are the life.
You are the green in the leaves,
The purple of the flowers.
You are the brightness of the sun,
The heat of the flame.
You are the breath of the wind,
The beat of a heart.
You are the flow of a river,
& the blood in my veins.
You are the way, the truth, & the life.

Creator

Lord, your majesty is displayed in the heavens,
Your beauty in the details of creation.
The sun exudes your glory,
The oceans represent the vastness,
& depth of your love.
Frequently I forget that you,
Almighty creator,
King of beauty,
Master artist,
Sculptor of all this awesome majesty,
Created me also.
Such knowledge is freeing & humbling.
I praise you, oh Lord,
Craftsman & perfector of all that is good & pure.
I praise you, oh Lord,
Lover of my soul.
King of my heart.
My creator.

Your Words

Lord, may your words dwell in my heart,
May I meditate on you all day long.
You are my strength in times of distress,
& your word is sharper than a two-edged sword.
In your words I find peace,
Nothing can shake me when I am rooted & grounded in you.
Meditating on you polishes my armour,
It reminds me who I really am;
Not just another person walking by,
But a beloved princess,
A fierce warrior,
A daughter of the most high king.
I am flooded with peace & strength,
You renew me.
May your holy words be ever on my lips & in my heart.

With Me

I hold myself tightly as I silently scream,
Tears stream down my face.
But still, you are there.
Through the pain & struggle I hear that still small voice,
'I still love you; I am still here.'
You hold my breaking heart,
You keep me together.
I satisfy myself with your words,
That should be enough.

Unworthy

I am unworthy.
Oh, so unworthy.
Still you, creator of innumerable galaxies,
Choose to reach out to me,
One of countless humans on this tiny planet.
You choose to dwell in my damaged heart.
You choose to flow through me.

Oh Lord of it all,
Burn away all the wickedness in me,
I don't want it anymore.
I want to be a place of holiness for you.
Yet I am so undeserving of this privilege.
Burn away this evil,
Let it hurt,
Let me heal.
Set alight that holy flame,
I want to be your fire.
I want to be a conveyor of your goodness.
Destroy this pride,
This self-consciousness,
This envy,
This selfishness.
I lay it all down at the foot of the cross.
The symbol of the price you paid to take this weight,
Off my shoulders, nailed to that tree.
Your life for my purity.

Flood my filthy soul.
Burn the evil from my thoughts.
Cleanse the sin from me.

Shine through the darkness in me.
Speak through me.
Use wretched me.
I am willing.

Jehovah

I carry your word in my heart,
Through the filth of this world.
May it keep me pure.
I meditate on their beams of light through this vast blackness,
May it keep me safe.

I focus on you while this world is shouting,
Pulling, for my attention.

If only the reward for wickedness was paid out immediately,
Oh, how unattractive sin would be!
How much easier would it be to see the filth of the world,
How much easier to determine right & wrong.

But you, in your unconditional love & mercy,
Choose to give us a lifetime to turn.
You chose to die out of unreserved love,
Even though we might not love you back.
What love is this!

I stay fixed on you through the evil of everyday.
Through the utter darkness of this world.
I hold your pure words in my heart.
I dwell on your words alone.
My shepherd, you lead me,
You hold me fast.
You have saved me.

I know my shepherd,
I know his name.
He is Jehovah.

& so, I follow.

Faithful

Oh Lord, you are faithful.
You are perfect in every way.
Your ways are just,
& your deeds, righteous.

You work everything for my good.
You can use messed up things,
Messed up people,
To complete your perfect plan.
Nothing comes as a surprise to you.

Although the destruction,
That man has caused himself,
Saddens you deeply,
You can work it all for the good of your people.

You are faithful in every way,
Your thoughts towards us are filled with love.

Remind Me

Lord may the ever beating of my heart always serve as a reminder of your goodness & faithfulness.

May every intake of breath & exhalation remind me of your closeness & love.

May every scrape & bruise bring to memory the atrocities of the cross – the great price you paid for my freedom.

Thank you, great king, for all that you are!

Life Song

Oh Lord,
Your majesty excels the heavens & the earth,
The praises of your people outnumber the stars.
Your glory is renowned in all the earth,
People long for you throughout all generations.

Let my life serve as a strong melody to your ears,
Let my heart carry the humble beat of my song to you.
May my words be as sweet praise & my breath as incense,
Let my soul silently cry out a beautiful harmony.
Lord, let my very existence be a grandly humble song to you!

Big Bang

Debunking the Big Bang Theory:
Nothing + nothing = nothing
Just like 0 + 0 = 0
Nothing cannot make something.
But even if there was a Big Bang,
We cannot make life forms on purpose,
So how could a bang of nothing create a perfect network of completely
functioning everything?
Where would the bang have come from anyways?
How can nothing explode?
How did the nothing get there?
It honestly doesn't make sense.
But still, I believe in the Big Bang...
...it was God's voice saying, "Let there be light."

How Can he Not Exist?

They ask, 'How can God exist?'
I smile & this is my reply:
Look at your cell's intricate design,
Your brain's perfect function.
Look at your heart & lungs,
How they keep you alive.
Look at the delicate maze of veins,
& the structure of your body.
The fact that you can taste, see, smell, & feel,
Your eyes & ears,
Your nose & taste buds,
How it all works perfectly.
Look at how your body heals,
How you grow.
Look at how plants synthesise,
How babies are born.
Look at how seeds develop,
& how caterpillars transform.
Look at how perfectly the sun is positioned so that we don't burn or
freeze.
Look at the beauty of the galaxy,
See the creativity of nature.
They ask, 'How can God exist?'
I smile & say,
'How can he not exist?!'

My Everything

To the only God,
Omnipotent, all powerful.
Jesus Christ,
Lover & redeemer of all his people.
Holy Spirit,
Helper & gift to the people of the Lord.
Eternal Father, Son, & Holy Spirit,
To you be all glory & honour.
The one who owes nothing yet gives everything,
The one who gives to people so undeserving.
The only God,
Generous & loving yet firm & fierce.
No number of words could adequately describe you,
All the languages of the earth are unfit for such glory.
Such love.
Not even one name is fit to cover all that you are.
My God & my king,
My friend & my judge,
You are life,
You are all to me,
You are my everything.

Idol

What's with the obsession of money?!
It is made to be a tool not an idol.
People chase it,
Hoard it,
But what difference does it make if you die rich or poor?
What can it add to the eternal gain?
Nothing!
Money; such a shallow purpose of life.
Such a waste of time & breath.
People are made for so much more.
I hope that one day humans wake up to all that they were created for.
They are missing out on so much!
Christ didn't give his life for us to serve the feeble riches of this world.
Wake them up Lord.

Thank You

Oh Lord,
The omniscient one,
Thank you for your faithfulness,
Thank you for your answers.
You are so good.
Thank you for building my faith.
Thank you for answering my prayers.
Please continue to grow my faith,
May I learn to trust you in every way.
In every day.
Thank you for teaching me,
leading me,
guiding me.
Lord thank you for keeping your promises.
Thank you.

The Broken

You choose the broken.
You see all our insecurities,
Our failures,
The mistakes we've made,
& the ones we will make.
I feel unworthy.
I break sometimes.
But you pick me up,
You never give up on me.
You see the most messed up people,
The most broken & wretched,
& you love.
You point directly at their soul & say,
'I love you.'
You see past all of it,
To whom you created us to be.
May I have your eyes,
That I may see the world how you see it,
That I may see people how you see them.
Lord, may I see past all their faults,
Realising that I have faults too,
& see who you created them to be.
Who you created me to be.
Give me your eyes, Lord.
May I love the broken too.

Enough

In this day & age many are confused
About who we are & what our purpose is.
We wonder if we are the wrong person,
The wrong era,
The wrong gender,
The wrong body.
We think God makes mistakes.
We think we know more than God.
We try to fix what doesn't need fixing,
We do what we weren't created to do.
We change God's perfect design,
In that way doing what pleases the devil:
Destroying God's perfect beauty,
Twisting his desires & plans.
It started in the Garden,
Where the devil first started whispering his lies.
"This isn't enough."
"I need more."
"I can fix this."
"I know better than God."
But most of all,
"Maybe God was wrong?"
We try find purpose in the mundane.
In belongings,
In fame,
In riches,
In things that are incomparable to our true purpose.
We don't know who we are,
Because we don't know the one who created us,
The one who gives us purpose.

New Every Morning

When conflicting & warring thoughts chase peace,
& sleep eludes my weary body.
You come like the morning,
You revive me & restore my strength.
Oh God, your faithfulness knows no end,
Your mercy & grace come new every morning.

Father

Thank you that you're not far away,
Not an angry God in the sky.
Instead, you choose to be my father,
You love me.
You are not up there somewhere,
Tut-tutting at all we do,
Or at all we fail to do.
No, you are close,
Healing us, loving us, forgiving us,
If we only turn to you.
Thank you for staying with me,
Thank you for healing me,
Thank you for loving me,
Thank you for forgiving me,
Thank you that I can genuinely call you papa.

Like You

I reflect on who I was,
Not too long ago.
I haven't been living for that long,
Compared to the human lifespan,
Not long compared to eternity.
But still I realise that I have grown so much:
I asked you for wisdom,
I am still getting wiser.
I asked you for peace,
It is flowing through me.
I asked you for courage,
I am becoming courageous.
I asked you for love,
It blooms within me.
I asked you for strength,
You are building my spiritual muscles.
I asked you for joy,
It bubbles to overflow.
I asked for your heart,
Now I know your love for people.
I asked for your eyes,
I can see people how you see them.
I asked you to be with me,
&, as I look back now,
I can see that you always have been.
Protecting me,
Guiding me,
Loving me,
Weeping with me,
Holding me,
& growing me.

Every important thing I asked for you've given me.
You've grown me & moulded me,
You are making me into your very own image.
Please continue to grow me,
Even when it's difficult to change.
I want to be more like you.

Desperate

Lord, this world is so messed up!
These people are so broken!
We need you desperately.
I want to give up,
I just want to come home to you.
I don't want to keep seeing all this pain,
I don't want to witness anymore horrors,
I don't want to see anymore atrocities.
I want to leave,
I want to come home.
How do you still love people!?
But then again,
Thank you for loving us,
Thank you for giving us more chances,
Every day,
Every second.
I know that I was broken too.
Thank you for your great mercy & grace,
May I be able to give that same grace & mercy to these broken ones.
These people who need you desperately.
Give me strength so that,
Although amid such darkness,
I might be a light,
That I might not lose hope,
That I might not give up.

There is Also Love

I begin to see that life is more complex,
& at the same time more wonderful,
Than I had ever imagined.
True, there is hatred,
But there is also love.
There is death,
But there is also life.
God has not left us.
He is with us,
Calling us to live the beautiful life of relationship with him,
Even when surrounded by an ugly world.

- *Inspired by Ernest Gordon's book, 'Miracle on the River Kwai.'*

Every Tear

I asked God to reach out to us in love.
When depression & sorrows seem too deep to bear,
When anger feels like a ticking bomb or a parasite eating away at us,
When guilt, shame, & the feeling of failing for the last time seems to
drown us in its overwhelming waters,
When pain, despair & grief is too heavy to carry,
When the shattered heart feels too painful,
When it feels too difficult to hold on.
He said to me; "You do it."
"This is what I called you to do."
To be the word of encouragement & comfort,
Saying, "It will be alright."
To be the warm embrace of love & peace.
To be the strong arm lifting others up out of depths of pain, shame &
suffering.
To be the listening ear people need to feel heard, understood &
important.
To be the fortress for people to go to in order to feel safe & welcome.
To guide people to find Me again.
To be patient, forgiving as I have forgiven you.
I will give you strength to do this.
I am your strength.
In my strength, go & be the person that the broken need.
I am using you to reach out to them.

Sometimes people are too scared to come to God.
Too afraid of judgment or religion.
But that's not who he is.
God is love.
He shows who he is perfectly through Jesus.
He loves,

He forgives,
He gives grace,
He gives hope,
He heals.
I think Revelation 21:4-5 shows his heart perfectly;
"He will wipe away every tear from their eyes," & "there will be no
more death or mourning or crying or pain, for the former things have
passed away... Behold, I make all things new."
So now, as God has called us to do,
We must go & love with his love.
Love because he first loved us.
Love because we love him.
Love because he loves them.
Love because we want to be like him.
Love because he is love.

Crazy Love

God's love can seem crazy.
When you realise that he loves you,
That he even died for you,
While you were against him,
When you ignored him,
When you disobeyed him,
When you made the wrong choice,
When you messed up again,
When you got it wrong.
He loved you through all of it.
When you realise how much you have been forgiven of, you really begin,
& only begin,
To see how much he loves you.

His love seems crazy,
Dying for the very ones who killed him,
The ones who turned their back on him.
But Jesus did it for you.
Because he loves you.
He took the nails agonisingly driven through his hands & feet.
He took the whips of leather, glass shards & metal splinters tearing the skin off his back,
Exposing his bones & muscle.
He took every painful breath where his raw flesh would scrape against the wooden, splintery cross he hung upon.
He took the long thorns pressed into his skull.
He took all the beatings & pain that made him look barely human,
Let alone recognisable!
All the agonising hours of ridicule, mockery, shame & agony.
He did it for you.

He could've called it off.
He could've commanded a legion of angels to his aid.
He could've laid low & rejected his calling.
But he saw your face in his mind's eye.
He sees you & says, "you're worth it all."
Such crazy love.
Even forgiving the very ones killing him & mocking him.
But his death wasn't the end of the story!
God brought him back to life after three days!
Death no longer has power over him.
Jesus is no longer dead!!
He died & rose to life again so that you might have a chance to come before God our father with confidence & awe.
That we might be able to have a relationship with him again.
He did it so that we might be made righteous & pure.
He did it so that when we come before the throne on judgement day,
Knowing our past,
But also knowing that Jesus paid it all & trusting him,
So that we can spend eternity with him!
We can have life abundantly!
He loves us more than we can describe.
This is all only a faint glimmer of the full picture of his indescribable, overwhelming, agape love.
This is only explained in human language with human understanding.
How much more glorious will be the full comprehension of God's love that will be revealed in our heavenly minds when he makes us new!

Who is This?

Who is this person staring back at me?
Who is this unfamiliar face?
Who is this person I'm meant to know so well?
Who have I become?
It feels like I've changed right under my own nose.
I want to go back & stay in the comfortable old me.
The carefree me.
Sometimes it's like I barely recognise myself anymore.
I don't know who I'll be tomorrow either.
I don't even know what will happen in the next second.
It all scares me so much.
But then I see him.
My creator.
I see him & suddenly it doesn't need to make sense.
Because he is with me.
Because he made me.
Because he knows me.
He knows me.
So, it doesn't matter if anyone else knows me or not.
It doesn't matter if I don't know what's going on.
He knows.
He cares.
He sees me,
The real me.
He knows every part of me,
Even the parts I don't know yet.
I don't need to impress anyone.
Only the opinion of the one who knows me,
The one who sees me,
Matters anymore.
My fears of the unknown future & unknown things,

All silence in his overwhelming & immense peace.
He knows.

His Voice

*I love the voice & the words that come from the very mouth that
breathed the galaxies into being,*
*That sends an array of seemingly conflicting emotions cascading
through my soul:*
Holy hate & deep love,
Righteous anger & pure joy,
Pain & overwhelming peace,
Despair & great hope,
Fear & absolute awe.
Emotions fill my heart & swirl in my mind.
*Just one word of his seems to stop my heart & make it beat faster at
the same time.*
His voice makes me want to sob & shout for joy all at once.
*When I hear his voice, it seems that the bustling world around me
goes silent as I lean in,*
Hanging on his every glorious word.
My heart swells.
I can never get enough of it.

Live

There is always a reason to live.
I know sometimes it seems that there is nothing left,
That there is no more to do,
That life becomes unbearable.
But there is always at least one reason to keep putting one foot in front of the other.
Maybe it's that one person,
Maybe it's the possibility of change of circumstances,
Maybe it's to make it to the next milestone, the next event,
Maybe it's for the next achievement,
Maybe it's to meet new people,
Maybe it's to experience more things,
Maybe it's to impact someone else's life,
Maybe it's to appreciate beauty & creation again,
Maybe it's doing what you love,
Maybe it's simply because your heart is still beating,
Maybe it's because it's not the end yet.
But I have the best reason of all.
There is someone out there,
Someone who knows you & created you & loves you.
Someone who knew you before you were born & formed you for a purpose.
There is someone who paid the ultimate price for you.
He didn't cause the pain of what people have done to you or haven't done.
He loves you.
Please don't give up.
Turn to God & be filled with his peace, his joy, his hope & his love.
Let the walls around your battered heart crumble,
Let him make you new,
Let his arms envelope you,

Let him be the reason you're still going.
Trust me, when all seems lost,
When it feels like there's no point in going on,
Come to God & it makes all the difference.
Find out who he is, don't travel life alone.
Keep living, but this time hand in hand with the very One who gives
life.

With Us

He lives among us.
He is with us.
Him, the creator of the universe!
He has called us his own,
We are not only his people,
But he is our God,
He is ours.
He relates to us,
He feels our pain.
He knows suffering,
He knows heartache,
He knows helplessness.
Because Jesus was human.
But the suffering of this world will not last.
He will wipe the tears from your eyes.
There will be no more death.
There will be no more heartache.
There will be no more crying.
There will be no more pain.
He will make everything new.
He will make things how they were supposed to be,
As it was before the fall.
He will recreate everything into his original design.
Oh, the glory of that day,
How we long for & look forward to it.
But before then,
We know that he,
The one who loves us so,
Is with us & cares for us.
So, hang on a little longer,
Through the agonies of this world,

Until the dawn comes & extinguishes the world's darkness.
He is with us.
We are his & he is ours.
Hang on to his faithful promise.

Love & Hate

If you love, you hate.
You hate the thing that destroys what you love.
You hate the thing that taints what you love.
You hate the thing that twists what you love.
It's impossible to love everything,
Because love without hate isn't love at all.
Love & hate come hand in hand.
God loves things the way he purposed them,
He loves what he has created,
But he hates the way the devil twists it,
He hates the way it gets perverted.
When God hates what the devil twists,
It doesn't mean he hates what it was before it was twisted.
Like sex,
It is a beautiful gift of God,
But the devil has twisted it into something perverted & far from God's
design.
Porn,
Rape,
Prostitution.
A thing used as a bribe,
A thing used carelessly,
A thing thrown around,
A thing that hurts.
That's not how God intended it.
He loves what he created it to be,
Therefore, he hates the devil's twisted version.

God made strength to be something that lifts up,
Not tears down.
Something used to protect & care,

Not something to destroy & hurt.
But it has been used to overpower others.
That's not God's design.
His design was something to lift up & support others.

God made beauty something to be treasured & protected,
Not idolised,
Not something that hurts others,
Not something used to elevate status,
Not something to disarm & lead others astray.
Beauty has been turned into a thing strived for,
That bodies are mutilated for,
When they were already fearfully & wonderfully made.
Beauty has been turned into something that's all outward appearance.
It should be about the beauty of a pure heart,
The beauty of a life full of the Fruit of the Spirit,
The beauty of a soul that loves God.
Beauty has been twisted into something that is ugly.

You can't love something without hating whatever hurts it or destroys
it.
Love & hate come hand in hand.

Children

I find that as we grow older,
We forget the little joys & thrills of living,
Of being 'child-like.'
We get so caught up in the pain,
The work,
The miseries & the difficulties of life,
That we forget the joys of it.
We forget to enjoy what God has created.
We forget to laugh,
We forget the adrenaline of running across a field,
We forget the joy of frolicking,
We forget to awe at a tiny bug or flower,
We forget to enjoy the sunrise & sunset,
We forget to make silly songs,
We forget to have simple & innocent fun,
We forget how to be 'children.'
But we are that;
Children.
Children of God!
Shouldn't we enjoy it?
Shouldn't we appreciate his creation?
We need to become like children again.
Let God be the father.
This sounds cliché but,
Life is for living, right?
Use what God has given you.
Appreciate & enjoy it.
Be the child you are!
Remember what it is to be alive.
Don't simply exist,
Live!

Let Go

I am so bogged down by thoughts & feelings,
By the confusion & chaos of the world,
By the brokenness of people,
By pain & heartache,
By the pressures I & others put on me,
By the stress of trying to hold everything together.
Then suddenly it all fades away,
As I see the one who overwhelms me with his love.
The one who surrounds me with his peace.
The one who gives everything away for me.
The one who knows my heart more than anyone but is still with me.
The one who's grace & mercy is new every morning.
The one who redeems me.
The problems of the world fades as I come face to face with his
beauty.
I am like a tree in the hurricane of his love.
I am drowning in the ocean of his grace.
The revelations make me want to weep.
He has been calling me to let go of all that had been holding me
down.
Calling me to trust him.
It overwhelms me.
I let him fill me up again.
I let him be my strength.

The One

I am there for everyone.
I am the shoulder people lean on.
I am the one who takes up the burdens of others.
I am the one there when everyone abandons them.
I am the one who's there when they need me.
But when I need someone, there's no one beside me.
Except him.
The one who gives me strength to go on.
The one who's there when no one else is.
The one who loves me unconditionally.
The one who I lean on.
The one who takes my burdens.
The one who is my example.
God, you have always been with me.
Thank you.
You never abandoned me.
You were always by my side.
Always lifting me up, time after time.
Always being my strength.
The world has taught me that the only one who is reliable is you.
I have learnt that if I rely on people,
It only leads to hurt & disappointment.
So, thank you papa.
I love you.

The Risk of Life

Anything worth having comes with a risk.
If you love, you may lose.
If you try, you may fail.
If you live, you will die,
But everything that matters is in between.
The heart-breaking grief you see at funerals is because first there was love.
But, despite the deep pain of loss,
The experience of loving & being loved is still precious.
Don't miss out on living,
Being safely curled in a cocoon but never emerging to experience the joy of flight.
Life must be seized without fear,
Or you'll never live at all.

Still There

I hate this frustration!
I hate these doubts!
I hate this struggle within myself!
I hate these inner questions!
I know, you're there, God.
Even if right now I can't see you.
I've seen your hand at work,
I've heard your voice,
I see the evidence all around me.
I know you.
But why can't I see you now?
Why do I feel so lost, broken, alone?
There's no reason for me to doubt you.
& despite the lies whispering in my head,
Despite the mocking voices praying on my weakness,
Scornfully asking where you are,
Despite that I can't see you right now,
I know you're there.
Papa.
God.
Father.
Lord.
I know you're there.
Because you promised to never leave me.
You promised to never forsake me. (Deut. 31:8)
I trust you even through my doubts.
Even though I'm frustrated.
Even though I'm struggling.
I trust you & your promises.

God, I know you're faithful.

I know you're good.
& I know you're still there.

He Knows

You can't say that Jesus doesn't understand what you're going though,
Because the very one who made humans,
Became one.
The son of God,
God's equal,
Became human.
He not only knows the human heart & mind,
But he has felt our pain,
He can relate directly to us.
Therefore, he can have compassion for us.
Not a sympathy that doesn't really know what you're going through.
No.
He walked to the grave in your shoes.
The creator of the universe.
The light.
The way.
The truth.
The word of God.
The very son of God.
The giver of all life,
Gave his life out of love for you.
You think a love that great,
That sacrificial,
Would give up on you?
You think a love that steadfast would be moved?
No.
For even if the mountains uproot & thrust themselves into the sea,
Even if the very earth beneath your feet crumbles under you,
Even if your world shatters like glass all around you,
I can assure you of this:

His unrelenting, never-ending, unshakeable, unmoveable, steadfast love for you will not give way.
Not only that, but through those times of fear in the immense destruction around you,
His peace will not leave you either.
He has promised to be the shelter in the storm.
He has said that his love will never end & his promise of peace will never be taken away.
He will not give up on you.

- *Inspired by Isaiah 54:10*

Moon Beam

I lay in the darkness.
Thoughts slowly creep in.
Dark thoughts.
Crowding.
Screaming in my head.
There's no light around me to scare them away.
I scream back at them in my head.
I try to banish them.
I try to command them to go.
I try to picture the light again.
I try to drive them off.
I wage war against them.
I tremble in the dark,
Alone,
Afraid.
The dark thoughts shout.
This is their domain.
As I lay there paralysed,
In the absence of light,
I find a beam of hope.
Just a singular beam.
I hold onto it with all I have.
The moon beam.
The reflection of the sun.
One strip of light across my pillow.
I lay my eyes in it & all the darkness in my head is banished.
A total peace fills me.
A peace so real I can almost feel it's softness.
I focus on that one beam,
&, although the darkness seems to dominate,
Against the one ray of silver light, it can do nothing.

I ponder in my now quiet & free mind;
Am I not supposed to be like the moon?
Reflecting the sun,
An example of God,
Shining light into the darkness.
Compared to the sun, the reflection of the moon in nothing.
But compared to the darkness, the reflection of the moon is everything.
I am supposed to be reflecting God's light into the darkness,
Into the screaming chaos,
Into the fear of the world.
I am supposed to bring the peace,
To be the calm.

I also realise that it's what you focus on that counts.
I could focus on the darkness surrounding me,
Crowding in on me,
But I choose to focus on the one beam of light & hold onto it with all
I have.
Yes, the world around us is dark & scary,
But choose to hold onto the ray of light,
God's peace that he provides,
His presence,
& the darkness can do nothing against that light.

Love Deficit

I don't want to live in a love deficit.
I don't want to search for love in the wrong places.
I want to be fulfilled by your love.
I want to stop trying get love from people.
But I want to stop feeling empty.
I want to stop feeling hollow.
I want to feel loved.
I want to stop living with a love deficit.
I keep letting people,
The things they think, say & do,
Break my heart.
I try fill my love tank with them,
But it's never full.
Because the only one who can accomplish that feat is you.
I don't know how to change.
I don't know how to receive your love.
I don't know how to get out of this love deficit.
My head knows you love me,
But my heart is not so sure.
Remove anything that blocks me from receiving your love.
Please.
Help me get out of this love deficit.

White Silk Ribbon

Sometimes I feel so down,
So empty,
That I just feel like sleeping forever.
Thoughts of shame & failure seep in,
Things don't make sense,
I don't understand,
The lines between wrong & right blur,
I don't care anymore.
I just hurt.
Everything hurts.
& there's nothing I can do.
Then I tied the white silk ribbon to my ankle.
I don't know why I did it at first,
But when I did,
It felt as though some of the heaviness lifted,
Like a fog was removed,
Peace & strength re-joined my soul.

It was a white flag of surrender to God,
Because I was so over the pain & confusion.
To me the white silk represented how he has made me white as snow,
How he has made me righteous,
He has forgiven & redeemed me,
I am no longer a slave to sin.
I'm not a failure.
It reminded me of who is on my side,
I'm not fighting alone.
Who created me.
Who I'm created to be.
I'm not who the devil tells me I am,
They were & are lies.

No, I am who he & he alone says I am,
Who he has made & is making me to be.
So, although the white ribbon of silk was like a cry of distress &
surrender to God,
It was like a war cry on the devil.
The silk ribbon doesn't have any powers,
It's just what it represented, reminded me of.
It shifted my focus,
Instead of listening to the lies of the devil,
Instead of believing those lies,
I focused on the truth of what God says about me.

Don't let satan steal the peace, joy & strength God has given you,
It's not his to steal.
Give God the lies the devil tells,
& the thoughts that are not of him.
Don't let the devil have a say in your life for another second,
Raise your own battle cry on satan's schemes.
Do it knowing who God says you are,
Knowing that he is with you every step of the way,
Backing you up,
Giving you strength.
Raise your white flag & roar your war cry.

Existing

I look down at my chest,
I see the beating of my heart,
I hear the thrumming of my blood,
I feel my lungs expand & deflate with each breath.
I'm alive.
Seeing the proof of life in myself brings some relief,
It brings some peace,
But some sometimes it just hurts more.
The fact that I'm alive.
The fact the I'm breathing.
The fact that I'm just existing.
Don't get me wrong,
I'm not suicidal,
I don't want to end my life.
Life is beautiful & it should be treasured.
But it hurts that I'm not doing anything with my life,
I'm just existing.
It makes me feel angry,
Helpless,
Depressed?
Stuck.
I don't know how to start living.
I don't even know how to live.
I sit inside all day.
I do work.
I draw.
I write.
But I don't do anything important.
I don't see people.
I don't make a difference in this world.
I don't do anything exciting.

What am I doing here?
What's my reason for existence?
I don't know.
All I know is that God exists.
All I know is that he made me.
He loves me.
& he has a good plan for me & my puny life.
Even if I just make a difference to one person,
My entire existence will be worth it.
So, I keep existing.
I keep breathing.
My heart keeps beating.
For that one person.
For the future.
For the person I will become.
Because he made me.
& he doesn't make mistakes.

Stuck

I love words.
I love how they can be used to express yourself,
To tell truth,
To show feeling,
To describe,
To love,
To comfort,
To tell a story.
But I'm tired of human words,
Human wisdom.
I want to hear & understand important things.
Things that will change me,
Heal me,
Improve me,
Make me better.
Things that will really help.
I know only God can do that,
I know I need him,
But I don't know how to get him.
Maybe 'get' isn't the right word,
Hear him,
See him,
Be close to my father again.
It's like I miss someone who's right next to me.
Someone who's always been with me.
I'm distant.
I hate it,
But I don't know how to get back.
It's like I'm trying to pull myself up a rope,
But more rope keeps coming over the edge of the cliff.
I don't know how not to do it in my own strength.

I don't know how.
I'm stuck again.

Something Good

The weight of failure.
The knowledge that I let you down every single day.
Over & over.
I hate feeling like I'm not doing anything with my life.
All this time & just...
Nothing.
I waste the precious breath you give me,
& in that way, I fail.
Everyday.
But I don't know how to do anything with my life,
I'm stuck.
I feel worthless.
I feel like I can't overcome this constant torment.
When I reach for your helping hand,
I feel as though our fingertips are brushing & I just can't reach you.
I don't know how much longer I can do this for.
Reaching, reaching,
But failing again.
I know you love me even though I fail you,
But I feel like my failures push you away,
Like they're separating us.
& I feel like there's nothing I can do.
I've tried.
But it's depressing,
Searching for some better version of me.
Just looking for someone probably right under my feet.
I'm so tired.
Tired of letting myself down,
Tired of letting you down.
Every night I ask for your forgiveness,
But it breaks my heart knowing I'll probably fail you again tomorrow.

It breaks my heart that I probably break yours.
It almost breaks my heart knowing you love me anyways,
In a way I could never return.
I'm sorry.
I know you love me,
But I don't know why.
I know I fail you,
I know I waste what you give me.
Yet you still love me,
You still forgive me.
You understand my confusion,
You listen when I call.
All I have to offer you is this brokenness & pain.
Yet you make something beautiful,
Something good,
Out of my life.

Wonderful People

I love watching people.
Especially my family.
Watching my mum draw.
Watching my brother laugh.
Watching my dad appreciate the beauty of the ocean.
Hearing my dad sing.
Watching my brother be silly.
Watching my mum paint.
Watching my family sitting at the table together.
Sure, it's fun to join in,
Laugh together & talk,
But I like occasionally stepping into the outside looking in.
Seeing them laugh, smile & interact.
It makes my heart swell.
I love my family.
I also like observing people I don't know so well.
Wondering what their life is like,
What's their story?
Watching strangers interact.
Watching lovers interact.
Seeing people laugh & smile when they think no one is watching.
Every unique person.
So beautiful.
Thank you, God, for wonderful people!

Little Things

The little things in life.
The things that fill the heart.
The afternoon sun turning the world a warm glowing gold.
The smell of the earth after a storm.
Leaves rustling in the wind.
Sun showers.
Sunrises & sunsets.
My chickens running for their dinner.
Golden hour.
Flowers in pavement cracks.
Flowers in general.
Fresh morning air & cool night air.
The expanse of ever-changing clouds.
People smiling.
People dancing.
People living.
Parents & their little children.
Warm breezes.
Everyone singing boisterously together at church.
Genuine hugs.
Making eye contact with that person.
Stars filling the sky.
Butterflies.
Finding another favourite scripture.
Candle flame.
The sound of rain.
A crackling fire.
Love, although it's not really a little thing.

Expectations

I probably need someone to keep me accountable,
But I'm already disappointed enough in myself.
I don't want anyone else to be disappointed in me,
To see how much I fail.
I know I'm not as good as I should be.
There are things I should do but I just don't.
There are things I shouldn't do but I still do.
I fear that I'll never live up to my own standards,
My own expectations of myself.
I fear I'll never be good enough.
I fear that I'll never be the person I'm meant to be.
I'm afraid that if I try again,
I'll fail again.
I'll disappoint myself again.
But I'll disappoint myself if I don't try.
I know you love me despite it all.
& I know you are making me into the person you created me to be.
But I'm still ashamed of myself,
That I can't do it.
But still,
Thank you for slowly transforming me.
Thank you for not giving up on me.
Thank you for never failing me.
Thank you for loving me.

Your Voice

I lay awake in silent terror.
A terrifying sense of foreboding smothers me.
The darkness seems so dark & deadly.
The shadows take demonic forms in my mind.
The silence is horribly loud,
But the creaks & scuttling sounds are not much better.
Dread & fear eat away at me,
Covering me like a suffocating blanket.
I fear sleep but I equally fear wakefulness.
I want to flee.
I almost reach my breaking point,
But then I remember your words:
There is nothing to fear.
I am with you.
No darkness can touch you,
You are mine.
Do not fear.
The shadows shrink away,
The darkness loses power.
Fear's hold on me is gone.
His calming voice in my head is louder than the screaming silence,
Louder than the creaks & scratchy scuttles.
Its ok.
I have nothing to fear.
You are with me.
I rest.

Haunted

I am haunted by my mistakes.
The things I've said & done,
The things I failed to say or do,
The ways I've hurt others,
The ways I haven't helped others.
I give them to God,
But they always come back to haunt me.
I try push them away,
But they don't stay away for long.
I know I've been forgiven from them,
They were mistakes & I'm learning from them,
But that doesn't seem to mean they aren't constantly whispered in my
ear,
It doesn't mean I can forget them.
I try to leave them behind & move on,
But it impossible when they cling to me like tar.
I can't seem to escape them.
I leave them at the foot of the cross,
But why do they return to my head?
Why do they dance like some evil cult in my head.
Mocking me & my failures,
Saying I'll never evade them,
That I can't flee from my own mind,
Reminding me of every little mistake I've made,
My every fault,
Every stupid thing I've done,
Every opportunity I've missed.
Please, help me escape these mistakes that haunt me.
Make them leave me alone.

Your Eyes

I want to hide my face from you,
To shy away from your bright perfection,
I want to hide my failure from your all-knowing gaze.
I want to hide my shame,
The ugly parts of me,
The ways I disappoint & fall short.
I want to hide my monstrosity.
I want to clean myself & perfect myself,
Before I stand before your glory.
I don't want you to see me this way,
Any less than how you designed.
I know that's not how it works with you,
I know I could never achieve perfection on my own,
& I can't clean myself - only you can do that,
I know you aren't put off by my imperfection,
But still, I want to tidy up my mess before being in your holy presence.
I know you're changing me,
Help me to see myself how you see me.

Lukewarm

I hate how I get comfortable,
Just chilling & living life.
I feel like I can't find that balance of enjoying life & serving you.
When I get comfortable not putting you first,
Having you in the background,
Not focusing on you,
When I get comfortable being lukewarm,
My spirit gets uneasy,
& I know I need to do something about it,
But it's easy just being comfortable,
Lukewarm.
It sneaks up on me,
Looking all nice & fine,
But I know it's a trick,
A lie,
A distraction.
It's made to make me feel like I don't need you.
It separates us in a way,
& I hate that.
I hate how comfortable it is to sit by & do nothing.
I hate how easy it is.
We are made for so much more.
We are made to be a fire,
Burning brightly.
Not sit like stagnant water.
Please, help me reawaken my spirit,
Rekindle the flame I know is within me.
Reawaken the lukewarm people of the world.

What I Do Know

There are things I don't understand.
& because of my lack of understanding,
Things I don't like.
Things seem to contradict.
I stress myself out,
Confuse & frustrate myself trying to find answers.
I ask people but they are only human,
They lack understanding as well.
I get overwhelmed & disheartened by my incapabilities.
I feel like giving up.
As I focus on what I don't understand,
I get bitter & frustrated.
But although there are things I don't understand,
I do know your love.
I do know who you are.
& I do know that you are good.
Although my confusion pushes me to give up & flee,
I am faced with the answer of Simon Peter in John 6:68:
"Lord, to whom shall we go? you have the words of eternal life."
I know this to be true also,
& so, I satisfy myself with what I do know.
I focus on what I do know & I'll find out the rest later.
Although there's things I don't understand,
I do know who you are.
I know you alone have the truth,
& you alone give true life.
Without you I'd be floating in a vast ocean with no land in sight.
Drowning.
Where can I go besides you?
I settle in what I do know.
I do know you.
The rest will come later.

Searching People

I see people,
Searching for love in places where they will end up broken,
In parties & clubs & the arms of those who never really care.
Only to wake up the next day & find themselves hollower than before.
I see people fighting for a distraction to numb the emptiness of their
existence.
Searching for fulfilment in places where they will not find it.
I see broken people,
Having done everything in their power to enjoy life,
Only to find themselves missing something,
Still longing for more.
I see people in agony,
Physical, mental & emotional.
Broken people who have lost all hope,
Ready to end it all,
On the edge of giving up.
I see people chasing after ambitions & dreams,
* only to complete them & find that they are still empty.*
I see the hollow hearts behind the makeup.
I see the deep agony behind the plastered-on smile.
I hear the sobs behind the laughter.
I hear their dying souls yearning for more,
Crying out for real love,
Longing for true purpose.
They don't even know what they're missing,
They just know they're missing something,
Often distracting themselves from the realisation.
I see them & hear them & I cry out on their behalf,
'Lord, reach out to the broken,
The empty, the searching.
Show them your love,

Your peace,
Your true joy & fulfilment.
Show them who you are:
The one they're missing.'
Thank you for breaking my heart with what breaks yours.

The Potter

My heart was hard as stone,
Cracked, thick, dried out clay.
But then the Potter,
My Potter,
Slowly softened this heart of stone.
Through songs, books, movies, words,
He convicts me of his great love,
Softening my dried-out clay of a heart with words of water.
Slowly he moulds my heart to be like his,
Loving what he loves,
Breaking for what breaks his.
I am no longer indifferent to the suffering of people.
I thought it was strong,
Not allowing myself to feel,
But really it was weak.
I was protecting myself by hardening my heart,
When I am made to have a heart like his.
& so slowly my Potter softens my dried-out heart.
Slowly he moulds me.
Slowly he convicts me of his great love,
& my heart can no longer stay hard in the presence of such love.

Light

We take light for granted.
When you're in it,
You don't notice it,
You just go about your day,
Unaware of the great gift it is,
Even as we soak it up,
Even as it sustains us.
But then in the darkness,
In the cold,
We realise the absence of light.
Its absence is felt so completely,
It's difficult to remember what it was like to have light.
Then when there is that dull speck of light,
Shining through the darkness,
It is everything.
We hold onto it because we realise its value.
Similarly,
We take for granted the goodness in the world.
& yet we realise the absence of it.
We see the importance of good when it's gone.
We struggle to remember it when surrounded by evil.
& the tiniest bit of goodness,
Contrasted with such vast evil,
Seems so good.

Who I'm Capable of Being

I know who I'm capable of being,
I know the kind of person I would be without God.
I know that if I harden my heart, I could become that.
But I thank God,
I never had to have a life transforming conversion.
I never had to be that person in order to find God.
I always knew him.
I always knew who I was,
Who I was created to be.
But people in my shoes,
Who never really 'strayed,'
Can fall into the trap of thinking we're better than those who have.
Because when you don't know what you've been saved from,
How much God changes your life,
You don't value what he's done for you.
& when you don't value what he's done,
You lose the point of it all,
You lose the relationship with your creator.
It becomes all about you,
Instead of all about him.
That why we need to know what we've been rescued from,
We need to know who we would have been without him,
We need to realise how much we really need him.
Thank God, I know who I'm capable of being.

Gain

Looking back on how far I've come.
I'm surprised at the distance I am from where I began.
It seems the miniscule baby steps I've made,
Amounted to more than I thought.
I hadn't realised how much I'd grown through unnoticeable
improvement.
All the mistakes I didn't realise I'd learned from.
Life lessons taken to heart.
How I've become stronger, wiser, smarter, softer.
A better person.
So many little improvements amounted to quite a bit,
& looking back now, I can see how far I've really come.
How all the mistakes I made weren't for nothing,
& the way I used my experiences, brought my gain.

The Same

The same stars I look up at & admire,
Have been here long before I existed,
& they will remain long after I'm gone.
It's comforting to know that,
No matter how crazy life gets down here,
Those stars will stay the same.
What I do won't make a difference to them.
I will be forgotten.
The worlds weight isn't really on my shoulders.
Indeed, it's a parallel to how,
No matter how crazy life gets down here,
God stays the same.
He is not shaken by anything this world could throw,
& therefore, I need not be shaken either.

Save Me from My Mind

I'm terrified of myself,
My mind,
My dark side.
But I can feel it creeping in.
If I were a pilot & a plane:
I can feel my controls breaking.
Flying in the beautiful sky was lovely,
But I fear that I will fall again,
Lose control of my plane,
Accelerating towards the ground,
Helpless.
I don't want to go back to that dark place again.
I want to keep flying.
But I don't know if I can help it.
I don't want to go back.
Will I survive another crash?
What if I can't bear it?
Lord, save me from myself.
Save me from my own mind.

Overwhelmed

Sometimes I feel a bit like David.
I have this great relationship with God,
& I am fully convinced of him & his goodness,
But then I get scared,
Emotions crowd in,
Cloud my vision,
I mess up.
The world suddenly seems more real than God.
I feel like I'm sinking,
I'm drowning,
There's nothing I can do.
But then I see God & I am no longer overwhelmed.
Fears drift away like smoke.
My mistakes no longer matter.
The voices in my head are silent.
My emotions lose their power over me.
Because his peace,
His joy,
His love,
His hope,
His forgiveness,
Overwhelms me,
Trumps it all,
Washes it away.
He is all that matters.
I'm going to be ok,
He is with me.

Hope

In the increasing chaos,
In the building fear,
In the mounting confusion,
In the dread,
The despair,
The anguish,
In the deafening noise of it all,
I hear a quiet,
& welcomely familiar voice:
Hope.

Validation

I'm always trying to prove myself,
Trying to convince others I'm good enough.
Seeking validation.
I convince them.
They confirm what I try so hard to prove.
& yet I don't believe it.
I'm always questioning my true worth.
I'm really trying to convince myself.
Will I ever believe I'm good enough?
Will I ever prove myself to my own self?
Will I ever meet my own expectations?
Or will I destroy myself slowly with my disappointment?
This is messed up.
Surely, I'm better than this?
I know I was made for more.
Help me, God.
Help me see myself through your eyes.

Be Ok

If it all hits the fan,
I know deep in my heart,
With full conviction,
Complete solidarity,
That I'm going to be ok.
Because God is faithful,
He is still good,
He is always with me.
I'm going to be ok.
Because I am standing on the unshakeable rock,
I am rooted in a firm foundation.
I can have peace in the storm,
Because God is my fortress,
My refuge,
My firm foundation.
I'm going to be ok.

Thankfulness

It hurts to miss someone.
It's easy to get bitter & depressed.
It's easy to cry in bed.
Refuse to get up.
But then I think:
Thankfulness in all circumstances,
Can take what the devil means as a weapon against me,
& turn it into a blessing,
Something good.
It's not always easy,
But when it's not easy is when it's even more necessary.
I wondered at how I could apply this lesson.
I am thankful that I have someone to miss,
What a beautiful thing it is to have someone to miss.
Thankfulness turns missing someone,
Into something of beauty, love, joy, peace, &,
Yes,
A bit of sadness,
Instead of something filled with anger, depression & pain.
The powerful weapon of thankfulness,
Has forged the weapons that were originally formed against me,
Into blessings in disguise.

True Worth

What determines someone's worth?
Their value?
Is it what they've achieved?
Their diplomas & certificates?
Their strength?
Is it their talents or abilities?
Is it what they look like?
Is it a scale of 1 to 10?
Is it what they think & say & do?
Is it how much they own?
How much they earn?
Is it how many friends they have?
Is it how many people know them?
Is it how much they've been through or survived?
Is it what they contribute to society?
Is their worth determined by what they think they're worth?
By what other people think they're worth?
By whom they choose to listen to?
Or is our value determined by the one who created us?
The one who showed us our value,
When he sent his son to die in our place just to form a relationship
with us.
The one who gave it all to have us.
He shows our true worth.

Fear

I am overwhelmed with fear.
Reasons for it are everywhere I look.
Fear of failing,
Falling short.
Fear of disappointing people.
Fear of being disappointed.
Fear of being let down again.
Fear of being hurt again.
Fear of losing those I love,
Not being able to save everyone.
Fear of not being able to be the hero.
Fear of not doing enough.
Fear of not being enough.
Fear of saying the wrong thing,
Or doing the wrong thing.
Or not doing the right thing.
Fear of it being my fault.
But then I look at God & his heart for me.
Because of him I don't have to fear.
He never left me.
He has never failed me.
Fear has no strength except that which I give it.
It has no hold until I give it one.
Fear is powerless without my contribution.

Never Given Up

I look at the world & see such utter brokenness.
People without God,
Without hope.
The neglect & abuse of the vulnerable.
The horrors of people in the result of sin.
Death & its effects.
The hurt people cause each other.
The pain of existence without meaning - emptiness.
Stone-hearted humanity.
It drives me to despair.
My heart aches for the pain & injustice of the world.
& I wonder why a perfect God would love us.
Why he has never given up on us.
Such love beyond human understanding.
Firm amid all this heartache.
There is hope through it all because he is still good.
Because of his refusal to give us up.
Thank you, God, for showing me your heart.

Indescribable Goodness

My heart is captured by the beauty around me.
Colours & mountains & trees.
The indescribable goodness & compassion of God.
It overwhelms me with peace after all I know happens in the world.
The horrors of humanity that break my heart.
That such beauty & goodness is not destroyed by the depravity of
humans & sin.
The overwhelming goodness, beauty & love of God.
Our creator.
I am given peace & hope again.
Oh, how God is good to me.

Love for the Lost

My God.
His great love for the lost.
His uncontainable compassion for the broken,
The hopeless,
The vulnerable & the abused.
Those completely at the mercy of those stronger.
How he draws us in,
Longing for us to know his love,
To accept his pure love.
To find the peace, hope & wholeness we're looking for.
The peace, hope & wholeness we so desperately need.

Such Love

Such love.
So vast I could run in any direction & never find an end.
So deep I could sink & drown in it for eternity & never find a bottom.
So high that I could never reach a top for there is no limit to it.
It crashes over me like waves,
Overwhelming me.
Yet at the same time it cradles me,
Wraps me up & holds me safe.
What is this love?
So beautiful.
So safe.
Everything I could ever need.
Fulfilling all I could ever want.
So perfect & secure,
Never ending.
Unfathomable & unmeasurable.
The love of a great father.
Undeserved & unmerited.
The love of my father,
My God.

Worth

My expectations for myself overwhelm me.
I can never measure up.
What kind of person am I if I can't even measure up to my own
standards?
I feel worthless,
Hopeless.
A failure.
The fact that I fail,
That I fall short over & over again.
I disappoint myself & learn to hate myself for it.
I have expectations for myself,
But where is my value when I can't meet them?
Where is my worth found?
Is it in my own righteousness,
Perfection?
Is it in my own abilities?
Or is it in the one who paid it all for me when I felt no worth?
Is it in Christ my saviour?
The one who claims me as righteous,
Who washes me white as snow.
The one who sees all my failures,
All my faults & flaws,
Yet still calls me worthy,
Still draws me in & calls me his.
Jesus, who says I am worth it all.
That's where my value should be.
He determines my worth.
& he chose to give it all for me.

Perfect Love

Why do I feel such fear?
Fear of being hurt,
Let down.
Fear of losing the ones I love.
Fear of my heart breaking.
Perfect love casts out fear, right? (1 John 4:18)
Only God has that perfect love.
Yet I'm still afraid.
When I know God's love,
Fear leaves.
But my old foe always seems to return,
Digging its claws into my heart,
Constricting my mind,
Rattling my soul.
Why can I never fully shake it?
It's always a conscious decision,
It needs to be a conscious decision:
Turn back,
Time & time again.
Focus on the love that casts out fear.
Is it that I don't trust God enough?
Am I relying on myself to control these things?
Is it that I try to find love in people other than the author of love?
Maybe I simply haven't grasped the full concept of this great love?
I know about it,
I understand it with my mind,
But my lil' ol' heart's still catching up.
There are moments where I know this love,
It overwhelms me.
Where fear has no place.
But I always seem to forget.

I don't know how to change it yet,
So, I'll just keep making the conscious decision to turn back,
Disperse fear with love.
I'll try my best,
I know God can work with that.

Pieces

Pieces of you are revealed to me,
They overwhelm me in their magnificence & magnitude.
& yet,
I haven't even scratched the surface of all that you are!
Its mind blowing that I can barely comprehend the most miniscule
part of God.
I think, 'Oh wow!
Now I know how incredible God is!'
But then I realise,
He is so much more than I could ever imagine or comprehend,
So inconceivable to my limited human mind.
All the majesty & bigness of God,
& yet he chooses to love me!
He provides every single breath I take.
That too is mind blowing.
Incomprehensible God.

Restored

I long for the day Christ will return.
The day when our sins & failures are removed.
The day when Gods creation is brought back to its former glory.
& yet I dread it too.
I dread that I may not have lived,
Or fulfilled my purpose.
But I find peace that,
No matter if I think I have or haven't,
Christs sacrifice means it doesn't matter what I did or didn't do,
I am accepted by God.
Made righteous by Christs blood.
I know that his timing is perfect,
& he is good.
Oh, I long for the day when humanity will be restored.

Grace

We could never meet Gods standards.
So, he chooses to restore us.
It's not despite how we fall short that he chooses to redeem us,
It's because we fail that he does.
Because we could never meet his standards by ourselves,
He chooses to restore us.
It's because he knows how helpless we are to solve our own
predicament.
He knows that we could give him nothing in return.
What grace.
Unmerited favour.
Undeserved forgiveness.
Unearned righteousness.

Growing Up

We're getting older so quickly.
We thought we'd be teenagers forever,
Always dreaming of the future.
We never realised the future was rushing up to meet us.
We dreamt of the freedoms of adulthood.
We dreamt about growing up & growing old.
We didn't appreciate the comfort of home,
Until we saw its end looming ever nearer.
We're teenagers trying to grow up.
Trying to prepare for something we've never been before;
Adults.
Teenagers trying to live adult lives.
How can we be ready for that?
We've been teenagers for seemingly our whole lives,
We finally figured out how that works,
Now how are we meant to be adults?
The future rushes up to meet us,
Time pushes us forward,
Constantly onward.
We're getting older so quickly.
It's exciting.
It's absolutely terrifying.
I have no idea what I'm doing...
But God does!
I've got God on my side!
So, I can face anything this world can throw.
I've learnt much in my few years,
& if I know anything it's that God's got me.
So come at me world.

In his Hands

Fear, fear, fear.
Constant voices in my head,
Am I good enough?
Am I doing the right thing?
Will this last?
Can I really withstand all this pressure?
Can I trust anyone?
Am I really worthy of love?
Are all the good things just a lie?
My future is at stake,
My world seems to be on the shoulders of my underdeveloped brain.
I feel alone.
All these decisions,
Am I making the right ones?
But then I remember,
I'm not alone.
It's not all on my shoulders.
The creator of the universe is by my side.
I don't live this life alone.
Even when I do make the wrong decision,
He can use it for my good.
I'm not good enough,
I'll never be good enough,
But he is.
It's not all about me!
My world isn't on my shoulders,
It's in his hands.
& I can trust him.
So, screaming fear turns into singing hope.
Peace.

The Tide

When I feel like I've been slowly,
Unnoticeably,
Floating away.
Taken by a tide.
Until I can only see you in the distance.
I find that I'm floating alone in empty space.
I can't touch the floor anymore,
I can't just quickly swim back to shore.
I'm lost.
Not only have I been disconnected with you,
But my family seem like strangers,
The people I love seem to be ghosts.
I'm disconnected from my anchor.
I'm alone in my head,
In this empty, scary ocean of a world.
There is no direction.
When I notice how far the tide has taken me out,
Panic grips my heart.
I hold up my fist is a desperate signal for rescue.
Then you're there.
You pull me back to yourself,
Back to shore.
I can breathe again.
I'm not alone.
You were always watching,
Waiting for me to ask for help.
My lifeguard,
My anchor.
Somehow, in being connected to you,
I am connected to the people I love.
Without you we fall apart.

Disconnected, I fall apart.
With you I'm safe.
But I must constantly be aware of my position,
My distance from you,
Constantly adjust to stay close to you,
Or the undercurrent will slowly take me with it as I enjoy my time in
the water.

His Love

I realised that's why God hates sin,
Because of the destruction & heartache it causes.
It's awe inspiring & humbling & uplifting,
That God would love me,
Enough to hate the things that hurt me,
Without hating me for causing them.
That he would love me.
Breather of galaxies.
Creator of mountains.
Painter of skies.
Knower of all my imperfections.
HE would love ME.

Great God

I look up at the stars,
Gaze in wonder at these innumerable twinkling balls of raging fire.
All the worlds & galaxies,
The universe you breathed.
I hear roar of rolling thunder,
See flashes of lightning.
Your power displayed in the heavens.
The vastness of the skies,
The great array of ever shifting clouds.
I gaze in wonder at your pure awesomeness.
The bigness of a God who cares for me.
My soul sings of your beauty & power & goodness.
My saviour.
My father.
My Lord & my God.
How great you are.

Creative God

Oh, you think God is boring?
Some old, outdated guy in the clouds?
You think God is dull & uncreative?
I see God in creativity,
He is nowhere close to boring or plain.
He was the one who invented creativity,
The painter of the very skies,
The one who carved the trees,
The sculptor of the mountains,
Filler of the seas.
He created all the things artists aspire to capture,
Re-create, convey, paint, draw, sculpt, photograph.
He is THE creator.
The master artist.
He is even the creator of those who create.
In that way we are like him,
Making beauty from seemingly nothing,
Conveying meaning, emotion, heart, desire, experience.
That WE are made in his image.
What a beautiful thought,
To be like such a beautiful being as God,
Author of beauty.
That we are his workmanship,
His prized & treasured art piece.
Such an awe inspiring & humbling thought.
That the creator of all beauty would create me,
To be like him,
To be his own.

Weary

I am weary.
I've been trying so hard to do my best,
To do the right thing.
I have no doubt that it's worth it,
But I'm tired.
The right thing is a heavy burden.
You help me carry it,
You help me handle this heavy weight.
You lead me in righteousness,
When I'm not sure which is the right way,
You guide me.
You give me the strength to carry on.
You give rest to my soul.
You're with me all the way,
Teaching me, guiding me.
I'm improving.
Learning to seek you.
Learning self-discipline & control.
Learning to forgive myself.
Learning to trust you.
You share my weight.
You are with me.
You give me rest.

- *Inspired by Matthew 11:28-30*

The Valley

I might be on the edge of falling apart,
Losing control,
Breaking down,
Giving up,
Failing.
But I refuse to be defeated.
I look to the God who never fails,
The one on my side,
With me in the lowest valley.
Even when my heart is heavy,
I will praise him.
Even when I'm on the edge,
I will not give in to the devil's tactics of depression.
I will worship the one who is good even in the valleys,
The one who lifts me up.

The Price

Jesus paid it all,
To cleanse me from the crimson stain of my sin,
To make me white as snow.
To bring me close to God.
He gave his own life.
& he says I'm worthy of the price,
Although I could never be worthy of it on my own.
The crown of thorns,
Nails in his hands,
Whips on his back,
Love in his eyes,
He says I'm worth it all.
Me, in my prison of shame & regret,
Me, trying to clean my own dark soul,
Me, in my instability,
Me, & my sin that keeps me from him,
Me, with my countless flaws & mistakes,
Me, in my doubts & fears.
Freedom has a price I could never pay,
Yet it's free for me,
Because he chose to pay the price for me.
Jesus paid it all,
Laying down his own life.
Now I owe everything to him.
For the crimson stain of my sin,
Has been made white as snow.

Amazing Grace

What grace is this,
To save one so undeserving,
One so wretched as me.
I was so lost,
Stumbling around in the dark,
But now you've found me.
I was so blind,
Willingly closing my eyes,
But now I see.
Despite all my failures,
You say you won't let go.
I still fall short,
But you call me yours,
Even though I'm so far from perfect.
I could never be worthy of this grace,
That's why it is that,
Grace.
Undeserved,
Unmerited,
Gift.
Such amazing grace,
To save a wretch like me.

Relationship

Why did Jesus need to come into the world?
Why did he have to die?
Now, most people would say,
'To take away our sin.'
Yes, but we're missing a crucial piece,
The why.
Why did we need our sin removed?
Because in sin,
We could not have a relationship with a perfect God.
That's the reason for Jesus,
To make a way for us to know God,
For us to have a relationship with God again.
Jesus' whole life pointed to God.
He showed us who God is.
Going to the cross,
Showing us the lengths God would go to,
Just to make a way for us to have a relationship with him.
That we could know him.
Showing God's heart for the human race,
How he would not give up,
Not let us go.
To make a way.
Just a way.
So that if we just reach out,
Look up,
Cry out,
We'll find him.
Because of his love.

Light of the World

The massacre of the baby boys of Bethlehem.
The darkness of the world that light was born into.
Jesus was born into,
For the love God had for the people drowning in darkness.
A light of hope burning into the night,
The song of long-awaited peace sung by an innumerable army of
angels,
A star guiding the way,
Prophecies,
Promises,
Fulfilled.
Generations of hope finally seen to not be in vain.
Light illuminating the darkest corners of hearts.
Light that no darkness could extinguish,
Not even a gravestone.
Lord of light,
Prince of peace,
Saviour,
King,
Born in a feeding trough.
Unforeseen.
Glorious.
Humbling.
Awe-inspiring.
That the king,
The light,
Would step down into our darkness.
That he would bring us light.
That he would care for us.

Unworthy

I'll never understand God's love.
How my failures will never change his love for me.
How I could never make it increase or decrease.
How is he not disappointed when I fall short?
How can he see past my failures?
How is the righteousness of Jesus now mine?
When I am so unworthy.
How does God love me?
& yet,
No matter how I question it,
No matter how I don't understand,
He does.

His Mercy is More

I fail again,
Fall short again,
My mistakes piling up,
But no matter how numerous they become,
His mercy is still enough to cover it.
Still never ending,
New every morning,
My slate is cleaned without fail.
I am washed again.
The stains of yesterday as if they never existed.
I am never too far for his never-ending faithfulness.
His mercy is always more than all my sins.
He is always abounding in grace,
Overflowing with love.
My sins they are many,
But his mercy is always more.

The Best for Me

You say you want the best for my life,
Better than I could ever imagine.
I don't know how that's possible,
When what I imagine is so lovely,
So seemingly perfect.
Yet you say you want so much more for me.
You say you have great plans & purposes for me,
You've made promises that I don't comprehend.
I don't know how they'll happen,
Don't know how to get there or if I'm capable,
Don't know how You'll use me,
Don't know how to make your promises happen,
Don't know the next step I'll take,
But no word of yours will fail.
You keep every promise you make,
Even when I'm unsure.
Even when I don't know how.
You will lead me,
You will guide me,
You will be with me every step.
May people be changed by my life,
May I leave an impact on the world,
No matter how small.
Use me, Lord.

Still There

I feel alone.
I can't feel you near.
I can't hear your voice.
I feel like I've failed you for the last time.
Like you've given up on me.
I know that isn't true.
You promised to never leave me,
Never forsake me.
I know you are the truth.
I know you are still there.
Even if I can't see you or feel you,
I trust you.
Because no matter what I don't know or don't feel,
I know you are good.
I know you are there.
I know you are faithful to your promises.
You are true to your word.

Righteous

I don't know how you're not disappointed in me.
How you're not shaking your head at my every failing.
How am I righteous in your sight?
I know it's because I am washed in the blood of Jesus,
But I don't understand how I can claim this righteousness that isn't
mine.
How can it be completely washed away?
How, when I still fall short of this glory,
Am I glorious to you?
How am I righteous when I constantly stain this garment of snow,
How can it still be clean?
How am I holy in your eyes,
When I can't live a single day without messing up?
Without putting my own wants first,
Without having a negative feeling towards others.
Although I can't seem to wrap my head around it,
I believe that you do still love me,
No matter how many times I fall short.
You do still approve of me.
You do still see me as righteous through the blood of Jesus.
Jesus' blood does not have an expiry date.

Last Enemy

I have held life in my hands.
I have waited hopefully for each breath,
Felt the warmth of life,
The relief of every heartbeat.
I have also felt the absence of life.
Cold, empty, lifeless void.
I know the pain when the next breath never comes.
The despair & finality of it.
Emptiness.
After hoping for that breath,
Reaching for that heartbeat,
Clinging to that warmth,
How could I ever bear to be the one to end it?
The one to steal that breath,
That life,
The one to cause that coldness.
We have the power to kill.
Even to kill each other.
Everyone has been hurt by death at some point,
So how can people not be pained at causing death?
The callous heart of humankind.
How it must break God's heart.
For he is the one who gives each breath,
Who causes the heart to beat,
Who warms each body.
How sad it must be for him,
The giver of life itself,
To see the very ones who were created in his image,
Supposed to have a heart like his,
Stealing the life he gives.
He sees each breath,

Loves each heartbeat,
& is saddened when it's gone.
His heart breaks with us.
But one day death will be gone for good.
The last enemy will be defeated.

Reaching

Once more I am slowly overwhelmed.
A tide of madness & insanity creeps up on me.
I am on the edge.
My mind is in chaos,
Turmoil.
Anger, hate, & terror drip from my pores.
It is the person I would be without God.
& I cannot hold it back.
I am about to tip,
Fall off the precarious edge,
Lose my mind.
I have cried out,
Calling for help,
But I found no solace,
No peace,
No rest.
It is only at the tipping point that I finally reach for him.
Reach for his word.
A last desperate grasp,
An action I should've taken sooner.
One I would've taken had the enemy not convinced me,
'They're just words.'
'It's boring.'
'I can make it by myself.'
I'd held myself together for a while.
Sort of.
But it hadn't taken long for me to start crumbling.
Again, I realise,
The only thing that holds me together is him.
He is my only peace.
& as soon as I reach, he is there.

Holding me together again.
He has listened,
He has heard,
He has been near,
& he has waited for me to reach for him,
While he's been reaching for me the whole time.
With me the whole time.

My Shepherd

I look at the raging, thundering, rapids of my mind.
I am chest deep in them.
I am overwhelmed,
Drowning,
Tossed,
Flung,
Flailing,
Sinking.
But then he.
He transforms the chaos,
Turmoil,
& confusion of my mind,
Into the quiet waters he leads me beside.
He gives me rest.
I walk through the thick forests,
Evil lurks there,
Darkness grabs at me,
But even in the darkest valleys of my mind I need not fear,
For even there he walks with me.
He sees my evil & horrors,
But he is not perturbed,
He is not phased in the slightest,
Not regretting his staying with me.
He holds my hand & walks through it with me,
Leading me to the green meadows on the other side.
He does not abandon me to darkness,
My own darkness,
But he gives me peace.
He will not cease his love for me,
Nor his goodness poured out on me.

He does not cease to calm the rapids of my mind & lead me beside quiet waters.

- *Inspired by Psalm 23:1-5*

Humanity

Oh, the conceited selfishness we call humanity.
The deficit of empathy in the human race!
You can confront people with the horrors & problems of the world,
Try make then face the facts,
Call them to a sort of action,
But they'll yawn,
Closing their eyes to that which offends their comfort,
Plug their ears & hum,
Reclining in their plush throne of ignorance.
Choosing to never dip a toe outside their self-centred bubble.
Refusing to let go of their naivety & share in fellow feeling with
another!
All they see are themselves,
Their little insignificant problems that they'll forget about tomorrow.
Why can't people open their eyes!?
Be convicted of the need for justice!?
How are people such strangers to empathy!?
The strong & the powerful laugh,
Squashing the helpless with a finger,
As though tormenting those completely at their mercy
Proves their strength & toughness.
You call this humanity?
Whilst those with hearts bigger than themselves,
The ones with the gift of compassion,
Feel powerless to do anything about it.
But God...

Beautiful Life

Oh Lord,
What a beautiful life you have given me.
Not a life without heartache or pain,
Not a life void of trouble & turmoil,
But a life where darkness makes the light brighter.
A life where ugliness makes beauty more beautiful.
Where sadness makes joy more joyful.
A life of variety & colour,
Dark shades that contrast the light & bright ones,
Making them stand out & become more beautiful.
A life full of beauty & joy,
A life full of hope & thankfulness.
Lord, you have given me the ability to look back on tough times,
& be grateful of the lessons learnt,
Be thankful for the beauty that comes after the pain,
The light of dawn that always shines even after the darkest night.
Thank you, Lord, that you have never failed me,
You never left my side.
Thank you for your faithfulness & goodness to me.
Thank you for this wonderful life I have.

www.ingramcontent.com/pod-product-compliance
Lightning Source LLC
Chambersburg PA
CBHW031931090426
42811CB00002B/143